Forever Breaking Strongholds

Written by:

Ryan Dickson

Editor: Patricia Barthwell

Cover Design: SOS Graphics Designs

Publisher: G Publishing LLC

ISBN: 978-1-7357302-6-4

Published and Printed in the United States of America

Table of Contents

FOREWORD
by Patricia Barthwell

I have known Ryan Dickson practically his entire life. I witnessed him and his siblings grow up to be wonderful, God fearing human beings, who would undoubtedly change the world in their own way. Ryan wrote, *"Forever Breaking Strongholds"* because of his deep desire to make his mark on the world. Here he shares the full scope of his personal struggle with a pornography addiction, in the hope that others will also use God's grace and redemption to overcome it. Many people have been plagued with varied addictions, a lot of times either through predestined genes or a pure curiosity for a given vice. For many, the addiction is simply something they fell into. This is what happened to Ryan, who developed his porn addiction innocently, at an early age. That dependence came to dominate every facet of his life, from his teenage years to adulthood. Ryan provides a lot of details to show how he dealt with the core issues of what he considered sexual sin, along with the shame he carried on a daily basis.

Ryan's true saving grace in conquering his obsession was recognizing he absolutely could not vanquish this alone. This is when he sought to deepen his prayer life, faith and knowledge of the bible and primarily his relationship with God. In this book, Ryan provides biblical references and tools he applied to gain freedom from the "monkey on his back," for most of his life. This personal memoir chronicles Ryan's life and the deep faith and arduous work that was required to claim victory. He overcame his pornography addiction and now wants to encourage and assist others to do the same. Ryan clearly demonstrates to his readers that if they lean on God, they can undoubtedly accomplish what seems to be the impossible.

We all are accountable for every word that comes out of our mouths. The Bible says, "And I tell you this, you must give an account on judgement day for every idle word you speak. The words you say will either acquit you or condemn you"
(*New Living Translation* Matthew 12:36-37).

Before the Father, the Son and the Holy Spirit, I take full responsibility for every word that will be said in the coming pages.

Chapter 1: Bob and John

Sin is sin. People can rationalize their sinful ways all they want, but sin is still sin. Even as Christians, we sin. We can't help it—blame our flesh. But there is a difference between committing a sin and being a slave to sin. For example, let's say there are two God fearing, Christ-believing individuals. Let's call them Bob and John.

Tonight, Bob is going out with some friends to celebrate his birthday. Bob rarely drinks. He can count on one hand how many times he's been drunk. But it's his birthday, so he thinks, "What the hay? I might as well have a good night with the fellas, right?"

Bob goes out and has a great time. By the end of the night, he can add one more finger to his count of how many times he's been drunk. Bob wakes up the next morning with a hangover and disappointment in himself for sinning. He let his flesh get the best of him. Before Bob started his day, he got down on his knees, and with his face to the ground, he prayed. He prayed to the heavenly Father with true sincerity and remorse. He asked for forgiveness, repented, and went on about his day. Regardless of whether Bob drinks again, Bob still sinned, according to Ephesians chapter five: "Don't be drunk with wine because that will ruin your life. Instead, be filled with the Holy Spirit" (*New Living Translation,* Ephesians 5:18).

On the other hand, there is John. Like Bob, he is also a man of faith. John, however, hasn't had a drink in three weeks. And if you ask John, those have been a hard-fought three weeks. It is a daily battle for John to resist the temptation of heavy drinking. His mind has become a battlefield. John is at war with not only his flesh, but also Satan, the greatest tempter known to man. John can't drink—not even a sip of wine—because John knows one sip will lead to a night of regret.

However, one evening after a rough day at work, John got the wrong call from the wrong friend at the wrong time to hang out at the wrong bar. And with the rough day of work sitting heavily on his flesh, John made the wrong choice and agreed to hang out with his friend. Then, just as he knew it would, it happened - one drink led to two, two turned into four, and four turned into a night of drunkenness. Three weeks of loosening the chains of alcoholism gone in an hour. A lot of praying, fasting and worshiping the Lord made John think the alcoholism was wiped away.

John wakes up ashamed. He wakes up mad at himself for letting his flesh win again. He feels like the chains he loosened are fastened even tighter than before. He feels defeated. He feels hopeless, like he will never be able to shake his addiction. John eventually gathers the courage to kneel before the Father to repent and ask for forgiveness. But even while he is praying, images of the night before are flickering through his mind. John can't believe what he has done. John is a slave to sin.

See, John used to enjoy drinking. He thought it was the best outlet ever. All his problems went away, and he felt better while he was drunk. The world seemed like a happy place. He felt more loved when he was drunk. He had more confidence. Most people didn't even know he drank a lot. By the world's standards, John is a "good guy." That was until John realized that being drunk was a sin and that God was displeased with him, each time he drank excessively. He learned that each time he was drunk, he was distancing himself from the Lord. Each time he was drunk, he was digging himself deeper and deeper. John was a slave to alcohol. His mood and life were dictated by alcohol. His addiction played a role in his divorce. Alcohol changed how he saw people. Being chained to alcoholism cost him a big chunk of his life; a life he was living in a darkness that no saved Christian man should ever live.

That was me, in a way but my name isn't Bob or John. It's Ryan Dickson and alcohol wasn't my addiction. Alcohol wasn't what held me in bondage for over 15 years. It was porn.

Chapter 2: Childhood

My struggle with lustful sin started when I was in elementary school. I had to be in fourth or fifth grade. I wasn't looking for porn and was never exposed to anything close to porn growing up. My parents had parental controls on my bedroom TV. My siblings and I couldn't watch R-rated movies, and I never saw magazines or porn videos hidden in the house. However, if children want to disobey their parents, they are going to find a way to do so, no matter what restrictions are put in place. The decision I made one night to defy my parents had terrible consequences and little did I know at that age, that it would cost me years of suffering.

When I was in elementary school, I shared a bedroom with my older brother. It was cool but sucked because when he wanted to go to bed, I had to go to bed, and when my parents said it was that time, it was lights out and goodnight. But one particular night, I wasn't having it. I wanted to watch more TV, and nobody was going to stop me from doing just that, so I devised a plan. When everyone was asleep, I would sneak downstairs and watch TV. I kept the TV volume super low and sat right next to it, so I could hear it. I just had to wait.

After staring at the ceiling in the dark, for what seemed like forever to me at that age, I gathered up the courage to execute my plan. My brother was a heavy sleeper, so it was no issue getting past him. The hard part was getting past my parent's bedroom. Their bedroom was right next to the stairs, so I had to be careful with each step I took. My heart raced, but once I made it downstairs, I was in the money.

I grabbed the remote and had my finger on the volume button before I even pressed power on. One important thing to note is that the TV downstairs didn't have parental controls, so all the channels were accessible to whomever was watching it. I really didn't have any idea of what I wanted to watch; I just knew I wasn't tired and wanted to be entertained with television. Clicking through the channels with no destination in mind, it was only a matter of time before I stumbled across something no child of God should see. Porn was just a few finger clicks away and sure enough it eventually presented itself. Live and in color there it was all mounted for me to see - there for the trapping. My eye gate opened, the demon entered and that is how it all began. Defying my parents that night was by far the worst decision of my life. If I could go back in time, I would watch myself sneak downstairs and I would pop out from behind the couch right before I got to that channel. I would give my kid self a whipping that I would never forget. Then I would go wake my dad up, so he could give my kid self a whipping as well, for the bible says, "Children, obey your parents because you belong to the Lord, for this is the right thing to do" (Ephesians 6:1).

I was watching porn as early as the fourth or fifth grade but didn't start masturbating until seventh grade. Like many kids, I was not a huge fan of going to school. At least once a week, I would try to find a way to stay home. I would play sick, pretend to be injured, and try to make deals with my mom. I attempted it all. Every once in a while, it would work. One particular day in seventh grade it happened. I was able to sell my mom on my not feeling well, so she let me stay home. I think she was too busy that morning to fight me on it, so she let me remain home - alone.

With the house to myself for the next eight hours, I could do whatever I wanted. For a kid, the day couldn't get any better. I could eat anything I wanted, play video games for hours, take a nap, blast music, and watch anything on TV—

including porn. Being a couple of years into watching it, I was able to find it on TV without having to pay for it. Once I did, let's just say that's how the masturbating began.

At my middle school, the kids looked down on people who masturbated. Kids denied it all the time. I was one of those kids who denied it. I would be made fun of if I admitted to it. And yes, because I knew I would be ridiculed, I denied even knowing what masturbating was. That was only partially a lie because in truth, I didn't know that what I was doing was even called masturbating for much of middle school. I just did it. I didn't know a name was attached to it but none of that mattered. I had a demon on me. Several times throughout the books of Matthew, Mark, Luke and John, Jesus cast out demons in kids, so when I was heavily in the sin during my middle school years, I figured I would be okay.

One day, a girl I liked called me out on my sexual sin during PE class. "You probably masturbate, don't you?" she vocalized, during a game of dodgeball.

"No! Why would I do that?" my mouth quickly responded, with a disgusted look on my face. But my body was frozen and in my mind, all I could think was, "Oh crap! How does she know?"

I remember the first time I was told porn and masturbation was a sin. I was sitting in on a Wednesday night Bible study service. I was in eighth grade. Most Wednesday night services have youth service upstairs but that night, I didn't go. I didn't want to go. Nothing in youth service interested me and really nothing at church interested me at all. I just went because my mom made me go. At that time, living for the Lord was not on my list of priorities. Sure, I believed in God. I accepted Christ in my life and was baptized around nine years old. I prayed sometimes, but as a young teen, I thought that was enough. At that age, sports, being cool, and girls were the only things I worried and cared about.

I ended up staying with my mom for the Bible study session. It was not where I wanted to be but it beat youth service, since that service required too much work and too much effort. In the Bible study session, I didn't have to focus on anything - just my thoughts. Whatever my imagination could draw up, that is what was focused on.

I usually liked to think about being an all star at football. Like most kids, I thought about scoring the game winning touchdown or how sweet I looked in my pads. Yep, this particular Wednesday night, Bible study was going to be a breeze. As the pastor was talking, my dreams were rolling. My imagination train was in full effect. That's when he said it. "Watching pornography is a sin!"

Instantly, conviction covered me. I don't know what the message of the day was that led him to say that sentence, but he said it multiple times and looked straight at me the entire time.

I didn't know how to respond and couldn't move because the conviction kept me motionless. I kept staring at him. I felt like I was the only one in the room. When the service ended, we got up and left, but this night was forever entrenched in my memory.

High school was a different breed. That is the first time I heard the term, "jacking off." Kids were blunt about the porn they watched. The words that are said in high school became the norm of everyday conversation. A person can get caught up in it really quickly, without even knowing.

I was walking in total darkness and had no idea. God's love, mercy and grace are some things I never take for granted and his patience with me, has me in awe to this day.

Chapter 3: Lust

At the core of porn is lust. Porn is not the issue. It is lust. The Bible uses words like lust, sexual immorality, adultery, and sexual sin to describe wicked behaviors people do, to defile their bodies and mind. When watching porn, all of these acts are committed. God knows all. Jesus, the son of God, knows all. They know all the wicked things that will be placed on this earth before we humans do. One hundred years from now, if Christ hasn't returned yet, I'm sure there will be other lustful devices out here that may not be considered porn. It may be called something else, but the sin of lust will still be at the core of it. So, although porn is what had me, lust was the main drive of it. Porn was the avenue I used to commit the lustful acts.

The Lord blessed me with one of the greatest treasures a man can ask for - a wife. I don't have a doubt the Lord was in the midst of us becoming married. God handpicked her for me and I know he had a plan for us both. The harsh fact is that my lustful acts destroyed our marriage. I was blinded by my sexual sin. Truth is, I thought that watching porn was not a way to commit sexual sin. The word lust is used so loosely in our world that the real wickedness of it gets overlooked. Porn is not the real enemy. It is lust.

Lust begins with dating. Where in the bible does it say we need to date before we marry? Where in the bible does it say we need to spend X amount of time with someone before we get married? Why have we created this human formula of steps that need to be taken before we marry? There are only two kinds of paths we as humans can take. The straight and narrow path to God's Kingdom or the broad road to hell. These two paths are outlined all throughout the bible and dating aligns perfectly with the broad road to hell. If God didn't say it, it's the enemy. If

Jesus didn't say it, it's the enemy. Dating is the enemy. Dating is fornicating. Dating is lusting. Dating doesn't exist in God's eyes. Boyfriend and girlfriend do not exist in God's eyes. We are either single or married. We are either lusting for another human or we are married to another human.

In the Lord's eyes, marriage is when a man and woman come together before God and confess that they will become one with each other. God says, "This explains why a man leaves his father and mother and is joined to his wife and the two are united into one" (Genesis 2:24).
And if we are married, we are willingly giving our bodies over to our spouse. "The husband should fulfill his wife's sexual needs, and the wife should fulfill her husband's needs. The wife gives authority over her body to her husband, and the husband gives authority over his body to his wife" (1 Corinthians 7:3-4). The word does not say, boyfriend or girlfriend.

The Word says "husband" and "wife." I was lusting for my wife before I was even married to her. God gave me this gift that he calls more precious than rubies and I spit on it. I spit on the gift God gave me. Not literally, but I spit on God's gift of a wonderful wife. Any of us who are dating are possibly spitting on a gift from God.

Before I was married, I lusted for my wife. Then when I was married, I committed adultery against her, more times than I can count. How?.by watching porn over and over again. Yes, I wanted to stop. Yes, the Lord had spared me and revealed to me I was being wicked beyond belief but the demon of porn still had a hold of me. This demon had been there since childhood. He made himself comfortable on me. He knew all the right triggers. He knew all the mental clips to play. He knew sounds to make in my ears. I was stuck. I was trapped.

Can I pause for a second and say, through all of my struggles with porn in my marriage, God still stuck by my side. He hated it. He was mad at me but he never abandoned me. Looking back on it now has me in awe. Wow! What an awesome God I serve!

Anyway, the reality is I committed adultery over and over again. The world doesn't see it that way though. The world thinks adultery is only when a person physically has sex with another person, while he or she is still married. Wrong! Jesus says, "But I say, anyone who even looks at a woman with lust has already committed adultery with her in his heart" (Matthew 5:28). There it is. Our savior has spoken. The world doesn't tell me what's right and wrong, The world will be judged and destroyed for all of the wrong it has done. I seek approval from my heavenly Father and the Lord Jesus Christ, who says lustful thoughts of a woman are considered adultery.

Is that not what porn is at the root. Think about it. Porn is nothing but lustful thoughts. Porn is nothing but looking at someone with lustful eyes. The world has many of us believers in Christ tricked. We are fooled. We are being deceived. We are being led astray down a path of judgement and destruction. And you can't stand before the Father on judgement day and say you didn't know. I'm warning you now! I'm shouting it up on roof tops. Porn is wicked! Porn is of the enemy! Porn is driving down the broad road to hell with its windows rolled down and music blasting. In the Bible, Jesus says, "Your eye is like a lamp that provides light for your body. When your eye is healthy, your whole body is filled with light. But when your eye is unhealthy, your whole body is filled with darkness. And if the light you think you have is actually darkness…how deep that darkness is" (Matthew 6:22-23).! Jesus spoke truth in every word that came from his mouth. For a long time and even in the beginning of my marriage, I thought all was well. Porn as a sin was not on my radar. I had been warned in my past but I didn't think much about it.

With divorce, we tend to look at the surface stuff as the issue but everything happens in the supernatural first. Whether you are a believer in Christ or not, everything starts in the unseen world. Demons are unseen. Lust is a demon and that demon toiled his way in my marriage. The demon did what he is an expert at and that is to steal, kill and destroy. I can't believe I allowed that to happen. When I realized that adultery was the cause of our divorce, it was too late. We were already divorced. I pray all who are reading this realize how destructive lust is. It will literally ruin your marriage and if it has, pray to the Lord for forgiveness. He is a forever faithful, loving and forgiving Father. I have heard people say they watch porn to keep themselves from cheating on their spouse because they don't see porn as an issue. They think it is harmless. If these are your thoughts, please ask the Lord our God to have a crop failure in your mind. That deception has to be burned out of you because these are the thoughts of Satan.

People close to us would have never thought adultery broke our marriage up. But I know it was the root cause of it all, brought on by my lust for porn. I gave Satan, the enemy, an entry point into my marriage. He took the path of adultery and caused chaos in every layer of my marriage. So naturally, it made it seem like our marriage failed for the same reasons other marriages fail. God knows our hearts. He knew my motives toward my wife were not always righteous. I had wicked sexual motives at times. It is something I strive through Christ to never do again. I pray all of my brothers and sisters in Christ Jesus will see the evils of porn and lust. If you allow it to, porn and lust will chew you up and spit you out. They will bind you up from head to toe and never let you go.

I feel the need to share...

There will be a time when each one of us is going to have to answer for everything we did. We are going to have to answer for everything we were supposed to do but didn't. Even our deepest thoughts will be held accountable. That day is going to be more real than any moment we have lived in this life. The scary part is once that day comes, we can't ask for another chance or a free pass. We can't cry, lie, fight, or buy our way out of it. We can't have our spouse, friend, or mom save us. We can't pinch ourselves to try and wake up. We can't yell, "Cut!" like it's a movie scene. We can't press restart like it's a video game. We can't close our eyes and wish it all will go away. We will just be there, exposed and waiting, hoping, and believing, that the life we lived was right in God's eyes.

I feel the need to say...

God is love, but He also shows His wrath and anger when He needs to. God is not just rainbows and sunshine. He is about order and righteous living. He corrects and addresses people accordingly for wrongful living. I believe this is a good thing. I would rather be corrected right away than continue digging myself deeper into sin. I would rather have God intervene in my life and get my attention than have my life go further down the wrong path.

Chapter 4: Receiving the Holy Spirit

The day I received the Holy Spirit was one of the greatest days of my life. It tops all the accomplishments and achievements I have received, and I wouldn't trade it for anything. Like I mentioned before, I was baptized and accepted Christ in my life at a young age. However, I didn't receive the Holy Spirit until I was 25. At that time, I was working the midnight shift as a supervisor for a trucking company. The job itself wasn't too bad. It was the hours I worked that I couldn't fully adjust to. I was always tired, even on my off days. Being tired for me meant more than just wanting to sleep. It also meant being angry and easily agitated. Unfortunately, my ex-wife was the one I took it out on, which is something I am sorry for to this day. She didn't deserve that kind of treatment.

It was Friday, January 19, 2018. I was just waking up from a nap after work. Napping was something I did a lot of to help cope with my anger and exhaustion. I remember my wife wanted to spend some time worshiping the Lord. This was not the first instance she wanted to do this. At the time, I was a lukewarm Christian. You know, the type of Christian who opens his Bible only on Sunday and really has no engaging relationship with God; the type of Christian who also has no clue he doesn't have a relationship with God. To me, the idea of taking the time to praise and worship the Lord at home befuddled me. I put up a small fight, but my ex-wife was persistent, so I eventually gave in. Sadly, I didn't do it for the Lord and I didn't give Him the glory He undoubtedly deserves. I only gave in so my ex-wife would leave me alone after we finished.

We got down on our knees. She turned on some worship music, and we began praying. At first, I was just going through the motions and wasn't really praying. I was thinking about how long we were going to be doing this because she could pray, worship, and read the Word for hours. I was so disrespectful toward the Lord at that time. I was awful. I was a hypocrite. I claimed to be a Christian but did nothing outside of church to build my relationship with God and I had an attitude when I was forced to do it. I was making a mockery of what should have been a sacred moment.

After a few minutes went by, I scolded myself: "Come on, Ryan! Pray and give thanks to the Lord for all that He has done for you."

Eventually, I stopped daydreaming and really started focusing on the Lord. It took a moment to get all the garbage out of my head and focus on God, but I did it. I just started praying and giving glory to God. At some point during our worship session, I felt a sensation for a quick second, that run down my spine. It didn't hurt but I had not felt something like that before.
.
It did make me pause. "What was that?" I thought.

I started praying again, and that feeling, that sensation, came back. This time throughout my entire body but my whole body wasn't shaking; it was more like a quick jolt. I was on my knees, with my elbows resting on the seat of a chair. The feeling kept happening, so I kept praying.

I was thinking, "Wow, this feels good." Then the music cut off.

My wife said, "Don't you feel better?"

"Yeah, that was nice. I needed that. Thank you," I replied. But in my head, I was jumping for joy and thinking, "That was frickin' awesome!" I don't know what God was doing to me, but I wanted more of whatever it was.

Around seven that evening, we needed to go to the store for groceries, so my ex-wife could cook dinner. The entire time we were driving, I was thinking about what happened to me. While in the store, I did what any mama's boy who had great news to share would do and called my mom. I rambled on and on to her about what I had felt while praying. I don't even know if my mom got a word in because I talked so much.

Once we were done talking, all I kept thinking about was that feeling and I just knew there was more to that experience. It was incomplete, and I had to get back home to finish it. I couldn't wait. I wanted to pray some more and feel that sensation again. I just knew deep down that wasn't all God had in store for me.

Once we got home, I sat on the couch and thought about how I was going to pray. I didn't want to mess this up. I decided to turn off the TV and turned on YouTube Music instead. I needed to drown out all possible distractions, so I scooted myself right over to the sound bar, got down on my knees again, and started praying. Sure enough, that sensation came back once I was totally dialed into the Lord. It got stronger and stronger until it had control over my entire body.

I have witnessed people receive the Holy Spirit in church. I've seen people fall on the ground and start shaking and before receiving the Holy Spirit myself, I didn't understand the magnitude of it. But there I was, lying on the ground with my body rolling across the floor. Thank God we had a big living room in our apartment because the Holy Spirit had me rolling everywhere. I was turning from my belly to my back and then from my back to my belly. He raised my back off the ground, so I was sitting up. Then he slowly placed me flatly on the ground. He stretched my entire body, with my arms pointed out and my legs spread wide.

I kept saying out loud. "This is awesome. Thank you, Jesus!"

I could feel and see everything happening but had absolutely no control over my body. It was like I was watching myself do all of this but from my own perspective. At first, I was so happy. I was laughing and thanking the Lord for giving me the Holy Spirit. Then, I felt sad. I started crying harder than I was laughing. I was crying because I realized at that moment how much God loves me, how truly powerful He is and the debt he paid for me. God could have destroyed me one-hundred times over with the way I lived my life. I wasn't worthy of receiving such a gift. I was mad just an hour before that, about having praise and worship time, yet God still blessed me with the Holy Spirit. I was crying, apologizing and asking for forgiveness for all my sins. God really does love me. I am a sinful man. At times, I am a willing sinner. However, God allowed this clean spirit to enter my dirty temple. I deserved none of that. I was sad for hurting God and displeasing Him with my lifestyle and the choices I had made.

At that time, I had just begun my battle with porn. I was trying to defeat it but was still watching it, since porn was still a big sin in my life. I didn't ask for the Holy Spirit, but God gave it to me anyway. He knew I needed him to break the shackles of porn and all the lustful chains it brings with it. God's love for me is greater than anything I can imagine. I need him. What an awesome God we serve!

Shortly after that realization, my ex-wife came from the bedroom, while talking to her mom on the phone. I was sprawled out on the floor with tears running down my face. I looked over at her, and she said, "Aww, Ryan just received the Holy Spirit."

Soon my wife hung up and joined in the flow of the Holy Spirit. All I remember is how we were facing each other and speaking in tongues. I don't know what the conversation was about but it had to have been an intense topic. We were talking in another language; one we hadn't studied in school. How awesome is that! I couldn't learn Spanish to save my grade and sucked at every bit of it. And I tried. Boy, did I try. But there I was, speaking in another language to my ex-wife. We were talking like we had done this before. It was insane. It lasted for a few minutes, too. Here's the kicker: I still had no control over my body. I was just watching everything unfold through my own eyes. I will say that the Holy Spirit likes to talk with its hands. I don't even have the words to describe the glorious things that happened after that. I've tried to find them, but all I have is this: God is good. God is love. If it was ever possible for a nonbeliever to experience what I experienced that night, that person would no longer be a nonbeliever. That was one of the greatest days of my life and one that I will never forget.

One last thing about that night. While my ex-wife and I were sharing that glorious night, I remember hearing someone crying. It wasn't me or my ex-wife, but I'm certain somebody was crying. It was very clear, too. It was like that person was in the next apartment over. Or maybe he was 500 miles away. The presence of the Holy Spirit was so heavy, that I don't doubt I could have picked up something that far away. I also believe whoever it was, he was experiencing the Holy Spirit that night. He too, was crying out to the Lord and was overwhelmed with His presence.

I feel the need to ask...

Have you ever been asked, "How do you know God is real?" How is a Christian supposed to answer a question like that? As Christ-believing people, we have to understand the person's intentions before answering that question. Is he or she a person, who is really seeking understanding and wants to believe or is this someone who is out to pick a fight? Does this person have genuine questions or does this person have an army of bad remarks about Christ, waiting behind that question?

I was put in this situation one time. I was asked that very question by a nonbeliever, who was not a knowledge and faith seeking person. This was a person who wanted to attack the Christian faith. Leading up to the day the person asked me that question, I remember the Holy Spirit telling me that I was going to have to defend my faith. The Holy Spirit flooded my mind with everything that had to do with my relationship with God, Jesus. It was at the forefront of my thoughts. Even when I was just trying to think about sports, my thoughts were interrupted by the spirit telling me I was going to have to defend my faith.

I remember the day clearly. It was my first week at a new job, and some co-workers and I were at work. A couple of us got hired together, so we trained together all week. Naturally, we built up a quick rapport. On this particular day, I was minding my own business and the guy who got hired with me, out of nowhere asked if I believed in God. He started attacking God and asking how if God is real, why He would allow certain things to happen. Of course, I stood my ground with the Word. We were going at it for a good five minutes. It got so heated that a supervisor had to come separate us.

The crazy thing is that I ended our "discussion" by telling him, "You don't know me, and you probably aren't going to believe me when I tell you this, but the Holy Spirit told me that this day was going to happen. The Holy Spirit told me I was going to have to defend my faith."

Of course, his response was a classic atheist remark: "Yeah, I don't believe that." I really didn't expect him to respond any other way but didn't have that "discussion" with him to amuse him. I think that was a test. The Lord prepared me in advance for it because God knew it was going to happen, and I needed to be ready for it. I just hope I passed in the Lord's eyes.

I don't want to paint this man like he was a mean or rude guy. He was actually a nice, respectful person but I would be lying to you, if I said I was comfortable around him. Before we had this encounter, I never felt right around him. I felt a disconnect when I was with him, as though he was lacking something. Like I said, he was a respectful and kind human being; I simply felt something was off about him from the time I met him. It turns out that "off" feeling was the Holy Spirit showing me his lack of faith. I know God is real because he speaks to me. He protects me. He covers me. He blesses me. And, most importantly, He loves me.

Chapter 5: Struggling

I find it very interesting that in Matthew chapter five Jesus talks about committing adultery with our mind and follows that up with talking about sinning with our hand: "And if your hand—even your stronger hand—causes you to sin, cut it off, and throw it away" (Matthew 5:30). Like many Scriptures, this could possibly have several meanings. For the longest time, I thought Jesus was talking about stealing. We use our hands to steal, right? Then I thought maybe Jesus is talking about physical violence. When it comes to violence, 100 percent of people use their stronger hand. Who fights with only their weaker hand? But now, I'm convinced that Jesus is talking about masturbating.

Out of my entire battle with porn, lust and masturbation, the most irritating thing that happens daily is how my eyes instinctively focus below a woman's waist, when she walks past me. This has become a habit, and by the time I catch myself doing it, the evil act has occurred. I wish this was something I never started doing and I believe it started in 4th grade. As sickening as that sounds, it's the truth. A demon has no care for respect or person. There are thousand-year-old demons lurking out here and the longer they have been around, the more wicked they are.

Now, some people say there is nothing wrong with looking, but according to the Bible, there is absolutely everything wrong with just looking. Let me remind you that Jesus said, "But I say, anyone who even looks at a woman with lust has already committed adultery with her in his eyes" (Matthew 5:28). I've given it great thought. My eyes dropping is not something I came out of my mother's womb doing. That is a learned behavior that has been committed literally thousands of times in my life and somehow seeped its way into a habitual reaction.

In the beginning, when I was submerged in lustful living, I yearned for a curvy lady to be in my line of sight. I could spot a woman walking to class and would pick up my pace just to get a longer look. I would make every effort to check out women. The gym was my favorite place to be because women in their leggings were literally everywhere.

Once the Lord revealed to me I was sinning, every time I looked lustfully at a woman, I ran from every possible temptation. For example, if I was in the grocery store and happened across a curvy lady in the aisle, I made sure I walked in the opposite direction. Aisle six was going to have to wait until the end. My once favorite place to be, the gym, turned into a gut-wrenching environment. I spent the bulk of my time making every effort to avoid looking at anyone. Consequently, my head stayed down the majority of my workout.

Speaking of the gym, here's when I knew there was a problem. This is when I realized I had looked so much my eyes naturally went to that lower area. One time I was in the gym working out and an "extra guy" was in there working out (It won't take long to figure out what I mean by "extra"). He had on some blue leggings and he made sure he was noticed. I didn't realize this was a dude wearing leggings until he crossed my path. Completely unexpectedly, he walked past me and there went my eyes. In this instance a millisecond felt like five minutes. Yeah, it was a horrible reaction. "Eww what are you looking at Ryan". A few minutes went by and I caught him off the reflection of three mirrors and there goes my eyes. At this point, I'm mad but I can't be mad at him. He ain't doing nothing to me, so I say to myself, "No more". I'm not about to look at this dude walking by anymore. To keep this from happening, I made sure I paid attention to the general area he went to, so he couldn't catch me off guard if he walked by. I would have enough time to force myself to look the other way. Several minutes went by and I had my focus back on getting in a good workout but sure enough, here he came strolling past me and there went my eyes when he walked by. I immediately got up and left. Yup, I cut my workout short. I couldn't do it anymore. Lord knows I don't roll that way. That was a big wake up call for me to get this obsession in order. If I learned this behavior on my own, I could surely unlearn it with the Lord's help.

So where do I stand with all this today? I would be lying if told you I am 100 percent removed from this burden. But I can tell you, I have noticed a big difference from what I used to be. I'm still a work in progress but am so grateful the Lord has been patient with me through all of this. I no longer want to do it, and it is merely a habitual reaction when I do. The thoughts of lust are no longer attached to it.

I feel the need to say...

God is love, but God also shows His wrath and anger when He needs to. God is not just rainbows and sunshine; He is about order and righteous living. He corrects and addresses people's wrongful living accordingly. This is a good thing, though. I would rather be corrected right away than continue digging myself deeper into sin. I would rather have God intervene in my life and get my attention, than have my life go down the wrong path.

Almost every day was a struggle with porn. It had gotten to the point where I didn't enjoy watching but still did it. Somedays, I just did it to get Satan and my flesh to leave me alone. Obviously, that's a terrible approach because they always come back. Somedays, I would be watching porn and literally telling myself, "This is stupid. This is dumb. Why are you doing this?" Then the evil deed would be over, and I was puzzled and disappointed about the whole situation. Somedays, I would just pay attention to more than the people in these videos. I would focus on the setting they were in, and sometimes, it was the most satanic thing I have ever seen. I would become disgusted with everything in the video. But the evil deed would still be done, and I would be mad at myself for being too weak to overcome my fleshly desires. I can't emphasize enough how wicked porn is. It is lust driving 120mph down the wrong side of the freeway and the enemy will paint the perfect scene like all is well. Little did I know I was headed for a crash and burn type situation.

Let me show you how this crash and burn ordeal looks in everyday life. One night, my friends and I were hanging out, celebrating one of their birthdays. I love my friends. I have the best group of friends a man could ever ask for. They are truly a blessing. One thing I love is that clubbing, partying, heavy drinking, strip clubs, and just plain recklessness are never on the agenda. Our time together consists of food, jokes, sports, and anything competitive we can get our hands on. I have what people call an "old soul," so it only makes sense for me to have friends ten or more years older than me. And as people get older, they turn in from a night out earlier and earlier, which means we rarely hang out past 11 pm and I love it because I'm not much of a night owl anyway. But on this particular night, I wasn't ready for bed. I wanted to hang out just a little bit longer. After some discussion, a few of us decided to continue our night of fun. We got in touch with another friend of mine, who was at the casino. Now, I'm all for the casino. I love playing the slot machines. No table games, though—that's too high a stake for me. This wasn't a night of slot machines, though. It wasn't a night of high stakes table games either. It was a night of temptation.

Forever Breaking Strongholds

The friend we were meeting told us to join him in one of those private rooms that has its own private bar and buffet. This was my first time going in one of these private rooms. After several phone calls and searching the casino floor, we found him, and to my surprise, he was with a few other guys and several beautiful women. They were all at a table, and it seemed like they were all having a good time. While some may not think this poses a problem, it did for me. There is supposed to be nothing wrong with men and women being at the same dinner table eating. But in my experience, when men and women meet up on a Saturday night and are dressed to impress, sipping on large amounts of alcoholic beverages, I don't think they are discussing hard-hitting topics like global warming.

Because I was in my battle with lust, the first thing I did was find an open seat away from all the action, as quickly as possible. I sat on the end seat, and one of my friends took the one next to me. A couple things were on my mind that night: lusting and trying not to judge people. I was in a situation where someone who claims to be a follower of Christ would quickly pass judgement. When I first walked in, I judged every man and woman there because there were people, who had no business being there. But Jesus said, "Do not judge others, and you will not be judged, for you will be treated as you treat others. The standard you use in judging is the standard by which you will be judged" (Matthew 7:1-2). I was not any better than anyone at that table. They were just letting their lust be known to the world, while I kept mine behind closed doors. It is still lust. It is still sin. But who am I to judge? "God alone, who gave the law, is the Judge. He alone has the power to save or to destroy. So, what right do you have to judge your neighbor?" (James 4:12)

Ryan Dickson

I felt out of place. Not because I was high and mighty, but because I'm never good in social settings. I'm shy and find everything funny, so I laugh even when I'm not supposed to. I also don't hold conversation well. The more attractive a woman is, the more I lose my ability to speak. To make things worse, I thought it was a great idea to have a few drinks that night. It was not a smart choice because it amplified all my embarrassing social qualities. When I really thought about it, I didn't want to be there. I was bored and nervous; if brought into the conversation, I would have either made a fool of myself or been interesting enough to any woman who wanted to flirt. I then would have to find a way to shut down every possible outcome, that didn't involve me going home and laying in my own bed by myself.

Time went by with conversations that I didn't include myself in. I kept my head down, eyes on my phone, reading the same football articles over and over again. Sometimes, I talked with my friend next to me, too. I could tell he wanted to go home, as well. After a little while, I thought we had stayed long enough where if we got up and left, it would be okay with everyone else. I texted my friend, indicating I was ready to leave, but I don't remember what he responded with or if he responded at all. I do remember putting my head back down, looking at my phone and wishing I had never brought up the idea of going out after dinner.

Right when I felt like everyone was ready to leave, more people showed up—not couples or a mix of guys and girls; it was more women. It took every ounce of my focus not to squirm and frown. As they approached the table, my heart dropped, and I just kept praying to the Lord, "Please don't let one of them sit next to me. Please, Lord, don't let one of

32

them sit next to me." While my soul was in panic mode, my flesh was licking its lips waiting to pounce.

There wasn't enough space for one of the ladies at the table, so we had to make room for her. While everyone was scooching over, I kept my tipsy self planted right where I was. She eventually found a spot and it wasn't next to me. I was safe. The good Lord saved me again, so I put my head back down, turned on my phone, and began reading the same football articles yet again.

The night eventually ended. Everyone was going to the next hangout spot, but my friends and I were ready to go home, so we did. Lust was in the air that night. There was so much lust that it got on my clothes and traveled with me back home.

Have you ever paced throughout your house, trying to get the urge of sin to leave? Have you ever just gone on a walk to talk and plead with the Lord to get those thoughts out of your head? Have you ever turned on a movie to distract your thoughts? Have you ever opened your Bible and read and read and read until your mind was at peace? That was me at 2:00 a.m. See, my ultimate fear that night wasn't sleeping with someone or making a fool of myself at the table. My fear was that the enemy was going to have enough ammunition to use against me.

When someone has the wickedness of porn hovering over him, a night like that starts with replaying everything that happened, including all the conversations that took place, all the food drinks, and the atmosphere. Everything that was heard, seen, or done gets replayed. No harm in that. But then those thoughts turn to what could have happened. What if someone said something provocative? What if this person sat next to that person or what if this other person wasn't there? Then those thoughts focus on the women there. What were they wearing? What did they say? Those thoughts then jump to women seen in porn that may look or act like the women there that night. Then those thoughts turn into dozens and dozens of images seen in porn, which create a desire to want to look up pornographic images. Then those images eventually result in action.

When that thought process starts, it is like fighting a losing battle. From a pure flesh standpoint, the worst part about porn is that it looks so good. Everyone in porn wears makeup to enhance her natural beauty, and you can tell each angle is filmed precisely to be provocative and sexual. Porn is lust, convenience, and secrecy at their highest levels. Masturbating to porn feels good too. Our sinful bodies love the feeling of sexual sin. They crave it. So, on top of knowing that God does not approve, that I would immediately feel guilty after, and that I would suffer a spiritual death each time I watched porn, I had to combat a transgression my body craved. That is the core of sexual sin. Here I am, living in a body that wants to do something that feels good. My body tells my mind that it feels good, so it craves more, too. Even when I can defeat my mind and my body, Satan comes in and tells my mind and body that porn and masturbating feel good. For the longest time, I didn't have the spiritual tools to defeat porn or maybe I just didn't know how to use those tools, God had given me.

I love what the apostle Paul talks about in Romans Chapter seven. He describes everything I was going through with porn to a T. He says starting in verse 14:

"So, the trouble is not with the law, for it is spiritual and good. The trouble is with me, for I am all too human, a slave to sin. I don't really understand myself, for I want to

34

do what is right, but I don't do it. Instead, I do what I hate. But if I know that what I am doing is wrong, this shows that I agree that the law is good. So, I am not the one doing wrong; it is sin living in me that does it. And I know that nothing good lives in me but is in my sinful nature. I want to do what is right, but I can't. I want to do what is good, but I don't. I don't want to do what is wrong, but I do it anyway. But if I do what I don't want to do, I am not really the one doing wrong; it is sin living in me that does it.

I have discovered this principle of life—that when I want to do what is right, I inevitably do what is wrong. I love God's law with all my heart. But there is another power within me, that is at war with my mind. This power makes me a slave to the sin that is still within me. Oh, what a miserable person I am! Who will free me from this life that is dominated by sin and death? Thank God! The answer is in Jesus Christ our Lord. So, you see how it is. In my mind, I really want to obey God's law, but because of my sinful nature, I am a slave to sin" (Romans 7:14-25).

The apostle Paul is the perfect example of who to look to, for all of us who struggle with addiction. For Paul to speak these words, he clearly had his own demons and was battling his own spiritual fight. I know my battle is the root cause of it all, brought on by my lust for porn. I gave Satan, the enemy, an entry point into my marriage and he took the avenue of adultery and caused chaos in every layer of my marriage. So naturally, this made it seem like our marriage failed for the same reasons other marriages fail. God knows our hearts. He knew my motives toward my wife were not always righteous. I had wicked sexual motives at times. It is something I strive through Christ to never do again. The Word of God is comforting because it contains a real-life example for every action a person has done and every thought a person has had.

Nothing is new to God. I am a living witness to that. I've
had some demonic thoughts and I've had some crazy
thoughts to try and counter those demonic thoughts. An
example is when I thought about becoming an "eunuch," a
word I came across while reading the book of Acts. I had
never heard that term before, so I googled it. I weighed the
pros and cons of becoming a eunuch - a man who has been
castrated. The pros were easy; the temptation of lust, porn,
and all sexual sin would be gone. What a relief that would
be for me. Women, as a whole, would no longer have my
interest. I could focus solely on God and doing his will.
The cons, however, included the physical pain of healing
after the procedure. I would have to come to grips with the
fact that women would no longer be a pivotal part of my
life. I would probably not marry again because what
woman wants to be with a man missing a very key piece of
equipment? There would not be a family, with my
biological children either. After weighing the pros and
cons, I decided that was not an option for me. But even
considering becoming a eunuch showed me how tired I was
of succumbing to porn. In the book of Matthew, Jesus says
to cut off your hand if it causes you to sin. He says it is
better to be missing one part of your body than your whole
body to be thrown into hell. It was plain and simple to me. I
thought about getting rid of my penis but I couldn't justify
missing out on a future, I've thought about for so long.

Spiritual and mental warfare in my opinion, is the hardest
war a person can be a part of. At one point in my life, I
used to look something like an animal. By that I don't mean
scary or frightening or literally look like a four-legged
creature. I mean physically; I used to have muscles and
work out a lot. Add in a decent diet and I was something
like an animal. Those of you in the fitness world know
what I mean. Anyway, with a decent diet, cardio, lifting
weights and boxing, I looked and felt like I could

physically hold my own with most people. If I were physically attacked by a person, I liked my chances of defeating that attacker or at least put up a good enough fight, where he would realize whatever the reason he was attacking me was not worth it. Even if I was physically attacked, I know those wounds will eventually heal. I know the pain I would feel would eventually be gone and even during that healing process, I know my wounds would bring attention to myself. They would also cause my family and friends' concern. They would see my bruises and cuts and want to protect me from another situation like that happening again. Being physically attacked is not pretty. It can be exhausting, painful and humiliating. Having said all of that I would rather physically fight everyday of my life than deal with a daily spiritual and mental fight. In a mental fight my muscles are useless. In a spiritual battle, all of those miles I ran mean nothing. That diet I was on, might as well have been an all pizza diet. All of that physical activity and healthy eating is as useful as a gun with no bullets.

There was a stretch where I was feeling good because I had gone weeks without the sexual, lustful sin of watching porn, but Satan was attacking me in my dreams. I felt like I had no control over the thoughts in my head. I would dream about things not even the best porn writer could think of. I felt helpless as if I didn't have a choice whether or not I could take part in it. I would wake up unhappy in the mornings about what I witnessed and participated in throughout my dams.

There I was, having what I believed to be a great day. I spent time in the Word of God. I spent time in prayer. I was carrying myself as a follower of Christ Jesus. Then I got home, laid in bed, went to sleep, and was immediately thrown into an X-rated movie. Sometimes, I would wake up feeling defeated, like I couldn't escape porn even in my dreams. I felt dirtier and more sinful than watching porn when I was awake. There were some nights I was afraid to go to bed. I prayed about it several times and even asked for forgiveness because I was the headliner in these dreams. Honestly, sometimes I felt like my prayers were not being answered. I know God didn't tempt me. The Bible clearly states that, "And remember when you are being tempted, do not say, 'God is tempting me.' God is never tempted to do wrong, and He never tempts anyone else" (James 1:13). But why was I still struggling? I mean, if I was able to resist porn before bed, why was I thrown into these sexual dreams? I would feel worse participating in these dreams than when I watched porn. Sometimes, I would wake up in the morning trying to decipher if I took part in it or not. Porn went from the joy of my life to the thing I hated most a guaranteed pick-me-up to my worst nightmare.

Now, there were a few times when I was placed in a dream that I felt I had a conscience. I knew where I was and what I was doing and would say no. I wouldn't participate, and the dream would be over. When I woke up, I felt good. I'd congratulate myself and say, "Cool! I am growing in Christ." I really didn't want this sin in my life. But most of the time, I felt like I was the main attraction without a voice.

Struggling can create doubt. Falling short so many times, displeasing God, and forever getting beaten down mentally creates doubt. It felt impossible to beat the lust I was feeling every day and being faced with the impossible task of beating lust made me doubt. I wanted to feel like Peter when he met Jesus on the water. When Jesus said for him to come, Peter had all the faith and confidence in Christ that a person can have. Peter didn't doubt. He believed his Lord and Savior could make him do what we think is impossible. No man has ever walked on water. But Peter saw what he wanted, and with faith, he went after it. He stepped over the side of the boat and walked toward Jesus. All was well until the strong winds and waves terrified him, and Peter began to sink. Why did he sink? Because he saw all the chaos around him, and that chaos caused doubt. That chaos made Peter think Jesus wasn't going to help him prevail through it. As Peter was sinking, he yelled out, "Save me, Lord!" Jesus reached out and saved Peter from sinking. Jesus said, "You have so little faith. Why did you doubt me?" (Matthew 14:31)

That is how I felt—like Jesus couldn't do what I felt was impossible. Through my faith, I was trying to heal from those lustful thoughts and actions. A second of doubt would cause me to sink, but still, I'm thankful because as I'm sinking, He reaches out and saves me from myself. Before Peter leaped out of the boat in faith, Jesus said, "Don't be afraid. Take courage. I am here" (Matthew 14:27). So, I had to tell myself the same thing; Jesus was there. Jesus was bigger than any problem, circumstance, or addiction. I told myself, "Take courage, Ryan. Your Lord and savior is here."

I feel the need to enlighten you that...

Sometimes we get caught in the routine of church. You know, arrive, sing praises to the Lord, hear a good sermon, tithe and go home. Sometimes we get caught in the routine of reading the Bible. You know, a good five minutes in the morning…. maybe 10 minutes before we go to bed or however long we can keep our eyes open. Sometimes we get caught in the routine of praying. You know, a quick prayer in the morning. A 2.5 second prayer before every meal or a half effort prayer before bed. Our walk with Christ can become one big routine. The hard part is, it can be difficult to recognize that we are not really building our relationship with the Lord. We are kind of just going through the motions. I am guilty of this. The sad part about it, at least for me, is it takes a crisis to snap me out of this. It takes a trial or two just to see how real God is. It takes chaos to snap out of this routine. We need to make every moment with the Lord genuine. We need to give him 100% of our focus. We need to build our lives around Christ and not have Christ fit into our lives.

Chapter 6: Temptation

Jesus was tempted by Satan for 40 days in the wilderness. 40 days! Satan just kept coming back with more and more temptations, and Jesus kept defeating them. "Then Jesus was led by the Spirit into the wilderness to be tempted by the devil. For forty days and forty nights he fasted and became very hungry" During that time the devil came to him, "If you are the son of God, tell these stones to become loaves of bread." But Jesus told him, "No! The Scriptures say. People do not live by bread alone but by every word that comes from the mouth of God." Then the devil took him to the holy city, Jerusalem, to the highest point of the Temple, and said, "If you are the Son of God, jump off! For the Scriptures say, He will order his angels to protect you and they will hold you up with their hands, so you won't even hurt your foot on a stone." Jesus responded, "The Scriptures also say, "You must not test the Lord your God." Next the devil took him to the peak of a very high mountain and showed him all the kingdoms of the world and their glory. "I will give it all to you," he said, "if you will kneel down and worship me." "Get out of here, Satan," Jesus told him. "For the Scriptures say. You must worship the Lord your God and serve only him. Then the devil went away, and angels came and took care of Jesus" (Matthew 4:4-11). That is some powerful stuff. Jesus was tempted. So, if Jesus can be tempted on several occasions, I know I will be tempted. We will all be tempted at some time or the other.

But I know Satan has never made me do anything, just like when Satan tempted Christ. Satan didn't make Jesus do anything. Satan just aligned everything so perfectly to see if Jesus would give in and praise the Lord he didn't. Nevertheless, Satan's tactics don't change. 2000 plus years later and he still approaches us all the same, including me. Satan has never forced me to watch porn. He never forced my head to turn and my eyes to dial in on a woman's figure. All of my physical acts have been committed by me and me alone. I have heard people say that the Devil made them do it, but that just isn't true. I can't find anywhere in scripture where Satan forces someone to sin. But what he does do is tempt us. Satan is literally a world champion tempter. Satan is the master of putting everything in the perfect place to get us to pull the trigger and sin. The main way he does this is by knocking on the door in our minds. He will always knock with temptations. It is his best way to get us to sin and the hard fact is we can never avoid this.

I don't really participate in the world of social media. I don't have a Twitter, Instagram, Facebook or Snapchat account. I didn't have a Myspace account when it was popular either. There are several reasons I don't. The biggest reason is that I don't care about what is going on in people's lives, and I don't care to share what is going on in my life. 1Corinthians 1:31 says, "If you want to boast, boast only about the Lord." Secondly, there is too much negativity on social media. People are mean and envy one another. Most people aren't happy for each other. Thirdly, social media is another outlet for Satan to tempt me to sin. I know because I have fallen into that trap before because we live in a sinful world.

However, I do enjoy watching videos on YouTube. When I was a workout buff, I enjoyed looking at workout videos. I like watching anything football related. Video games, movie clips, and cars also pique my interest. As long as I stay away from the comment section that is riddled with negative remarks, I am good.

While I was knee deep in sexual sin, YouTube became like a softcore porn site for me. Football became the "lingerie football league." Movie clips turned into sex scenes from every movie. Car videos turned into models in short skirts showing off their "cars". My workout videos turned into squat day with the "see-through leggings girl." It was terrible. I was ashamed to pull up YouTube on my phone around people because I knew my recommended videos were littered with filth. Once I was ready to defeat sexual sin in my life, it took weeks to get that stuff removed. I even gave a thumbs down and red flags and clicked the "not interested" button on many videos. I could have made a new account and am not sure why I didn't. But after some time, I eventually got my account looking like I was just a person, who was truly interested in sports, cars, and video games.

However, Satan will use anything to get our attention, especially something he knows has caused us to sin previously. Ever so often, when I go on YouTube, a clip of temptation will pop up on my feed: "Butt blaster day with Jane Doe" or, "Women's beach volleyball quarter finals".

Now, Jane Doe could be an expert on targeting all the muscles on the human butt. She could have all the best tips and tricks to getting the best results but I know that if I click on this video, I am opening the door for temptation. I am letting temptation in, and it is going to be a battle to get it to leave. And if I ignore the knocking, it will continue to knock until I open the door or kick it off my front porch. So, rather than letting it in to wreak havoc on my life, I kick it off my front porch and click "not interested," so the video will go away. I could play dumb and think that YouTube was simply recommending a video it thought I would like because I watch a lot of workout videos. However, there is no way I could apply that foolish way of thinking when it comes to women's beach volleyball. Even though volleyball was one of my favorite sports to play in gym class when I was growing up, I have never watched any video related to volleyball, especially women's beach volleyball. I have never even been to a beach. How does YouTube think this video is something I would be interested in? The answer is it doesn't. It is a temptation by Satan.

Chapter 7: My Salvation

My salvation is everything to me. It is a gift that I surely don't deserve. Paul said, "Salvation is not a reward for the good things we have done, so none of us can boast about it" (Ephesians 2:9). For the longest time, I didn't fully understand what salvation means. I have heard it in church and friends and family have brought it up in conversation, but I never cared enough to ask or look up the definition of salvation.

After spending some time in the Word, I started to grasp the full meaning of salvation. It is another example of love and grace God shows us. I have intentionally sinned hundreds of times and have made promises to God that I have failed to hold true. I have ignored, hidden from, and been mad at Him, yet the fact that He still loves me through all of that is too much for a human brain to understand. I would be lost or dead if it wasn't for God's love.

Although, something has been nagging at me, as I learn more about God and His love. Can I lose my salvation? If I continue to lust and indulge in sexual immorality and sin, can I fall away from God? What if I'm intentionally doing it? Or what if I know it's wrong but am too weak to break from its shackles? The answer is yes! We can lose our salvation if we are living our lives in sin...porn included. Let's look at two particular Scriptures that strike the fear of God in me and they both are in the book of Matthew. The first says, "You can enter God's Kingdom only through the narrow gate. The highway to hell is broad, and its gate is wide for the many who choose that way. But the gateway to life is very narrow, and the road is difficult, and only a few ever find it" (Matthew 7:13-14). I have been told this scripture really is talking about Christ. People have said it means some will choose not to believe in Christ, and that road is wide because there are many who don't and there is only a small portion of people, who believe in Christ, so that is why the gate is narrow. That could very well be true. I am still young in my faith, so I am open to listening to all healthy interpretations of the Word. But I think the Word is as straightforward as much as it contains deeper meanings. By that, I mean that the words we are reading mean exactly what they say, even though we can take them to mean more. It is hard to enter God's Kingdom. The gate is not narrow because many will not believe in Christ. It is narrow because it is difficult to not only believe in Christ but also to follow him. The path to hell is wide because many will choose not to follow Christ. That is what I understood when I read that passage. God isn't trying to trick us, and Jesus is not trying to deceive us; He is trying to get us to understand.

The second Scripture that has God's fear pouring through me is, "Not everyone who calls out to me, 'Lord! Lord!' will enter the Kingdom of Heaven. Only those who actually do the will of my Father in Heaven will enter. On Judgement day, many will say to me, 'Lord! Lord! We prophesied in your name and performed many miracles in your name.' But I will reply, 'I never knew you. Get away from me, you who break God's Law" (Matthew 7:21-23). Every time I read that scripture, I tell myself, "Ryan, you have to get it together. Eternity is a long time." When I really break this passage down, it is eye opening. The people mentioned clearly knew of Jesus. They recognized His great power and helped people, according to them. They say they performed miracles, meaning they healed people in the name of Jesus. The King James Version says they cast devils out in His name and did many wonderful works in His name. These works and miracles that these people say they performed, still weren't enough because they disobeyed God. They did evil too. They did not bear good fruit. Their lives were not in line with doing the will of God. Their lives were divided between good and evil. Surely, they knew the Lord's name but demons know Jesus. The bible says, "that at the name of Jesus every knee should bow, in heaven and on earth and under the earth, and every tongue declare that Jesus Christ is Lord, to the glory of God the Father" (Philippians 2:10-11). We can't just say we believe in Jesus but live a life that is the complete opposite of his ministry. That doesn't add up "You cannot eat at the Lord's Table and at the table of demons, too" (1 Corinthians 10:21). I would argue that demons know Jesus better than some of us as believers do but I will leave that topic for another day.

I have read articles and listened to different pastors trying to break these Scriptures down, and none of what they say makes sense to me. I don't like when people try to sugarcoat the Word of God. They try to make it seem like there are no consequences, correction, or punishment in Scripture. But what really irritates me is when people use a verse to trump another verse to justify the point they are trying to get across. Isn't every word in the Bible of importance? Why would it be in the Bible if it wasn't? The Word is God. Also, if Jesus said it, wouldn't that make it that much more important?

Wait! There is a third scripture that came to me. "Anyone who does not remain in me is thrown away like a useless branch and withers. Such branches are gathered into a pile to be burned. But if you remain in me and my words remain in you, you may ask for anything you desire and it will be granted" (John 15: 6-7). That was also Jesus speaking by the way.

So if I'm knee deep in porn, how am I remaining in Christ? This is something I toiled with for a very long time. Where in the Bible does it say, you will still enter the Kingdom even if you have lust attached to your soul? All I see is a number of warnings the apostle Paul gives to several churches. "When you follow the desires of your sinful nature, the results are very clear: sexual immorality, impurity, lustful pleasures, idolatry, sorcery, hostility, quarreling, jealousy, outbursts of anger, selfish ambition, dissension, division, envy, drunkenness, wild parties, and other sins like these. Let me tell you again, as I have before, that anyone living that sort of life will not inherit the Kingdom of God" (Galatians 5:19-21).

Here is another warning from the Lord. "Let there be no sexual immorality, impurity, or greed among you. Such sins have no place among God's people. Obscene stories, foolish talk, and coarse jokes—these are not for you. Instead, let there be thankfulness to God. You can be sure that no immoral, impure, or greedy person will inherit the Kingdom of God. For a greedy person is an idolater, worshiping the things of this world" (Ephesians 5:3-5).

And another warning from the Apostle Paul - "Run from sexual sin! No other sin so clearly affects the body as this one does. For sexual immorality is a sin against your own body. Don't you realize that your body is the temple of the Holy Spirit, who lives in you and was given to you by God? You do not belong to yourself, for God bought you with a high price. So, you must honor God with your body" (1 Corinthians 6:18-20). How can I dirty God's House (my body) and I don't even own my own body. God paid a high price for my body, with his one and only Son, Jesus Christ. So what right do I have to damage someone else's property? I'm just renting.

One last Scripture, "Because we belong to the day, we must live decent lives for all to see. Don't participate in the darkness of wild parties and drunkenness, or in sexual promiscuity and immoral living, or in quarreling and jealousy" (Romans 13:13). These are the same warnings over and over again and this is just from the New Testament. The same warnings are also stated throughout the Old testament.

Am I not part of the church? I pray I am. I hope I am. Apparently the apostle Paul is warning me! He's warning all of us, who surrender to lust. I had to break free from porn. God doesn't play. God doesn't mix or waste words. And when God repeats himself, we need to listen. If God says lust in the mind is wicked and those who do it will be judged and pay great consequences for it, how can I continue to do it? How can I continue to live in porn?

 I knew Jesus was eventually going to heal me from it. Jesus says, "For my yoke is easy to bear, and the burden I give is light" (Matthew 11:30). The Word also says, "Give all your worries and cares to God, for he cares about you" (1 Peter 5:7). I read these verses and prayed these prayers many times to God. If Jesus can heal the sick, if He can cure the wicked, if He can walk on water, if He can defeat death, then how can He not deliver me from porn? "The temptations in your life are no different from what others experience. And God is faithful. He will not allow the temptation to be more than you can stand. When you are tempted, He will show you a way out so you can endure" (1 Corinthians 10:13). Praise God for his faithfulness because without Him I would still be drowning in porn. I give all credit to Him but I had to want to change. I had to want to make the sacrifices to be set free. And if I didn't want to change but still claim Jesus as my Lord and Savior, I would only be fooling myself.

But hold on before you stop reading because I've got one more. "Dear friends, if we deliberately continue sinning after we have received knowledge of the truth, there is no longer any sacrifice that will cover these sins. There is only the terrible expectation of God's judgement and the raging fire that will consume his enemies. For anyone who refused to obey the law of Moses was put to death without mercy, on the testimony of two or three witnesses. Just think how much worse the punishment will be for those who have trampled on the Son of God" (Hebrews 10:26-29, NLT). You can read that in any Bible translation you want and it is still going to mean the same thing. There is no way I read these verses over and over again and not have the fear of God grip me. The Bible says, "Serve the Lord with reverent fear, and rejoice with trembling" (Psalms 2:11). To fear God means to hate sin. To fear God means to hate evil. To fear God means following his commands. Porn is not doing any of these things. Porn is sin, porn is evil and porn is certainly breaking God's commands.

Also, who are these warnings and teachings being directed to? No matter what a person's belief of salvation is, I think we can all agree that the foundation of being saved is accepting and believing that Jesus Christ is the Son of God and that He came to earth, died for our sins, and rose from the dead on the third day. All that is the fundamental key to being saved right? So, in all of these verses where Jesus or the apostle Paul is talking and giving us warning and direction on how to live and not to live, who are they talking to? They can't be talking to those who don't believe that Jesus is the Messiah and the Son of the Living God because those people don't believe the most important thing a person needs to believe, in order to be saved. This must mean that they are talking to those of us who have accepted Christ in our lives. "Don't you realize that those who do wrong will not inherit the kingdom of God? Don't fool yourselves. Those who indulge in sexual sin, or worship idols, or commit adultery, or prostitute themselves, or practice homosexuality, or are thieves or greedy people or drunkards, or are abusive or cheat —none of these people will inherit the Kingdom of God" (1 Corinthians 6:9-10).

However, I wouldn't tell a fellow born-again believer that he could lose his salvation. I wouldn't dare tell him that if he continues living a life of intentional and willing sin, he will fall out of his walk with Christ. Who am I to say that to someone? I am in no position to judge or condemn anyone. I am fighting my own spiritual battles, which I have lost my fair share of. On the flip side, I will also never celebrate a born-again believer, who is deliberately sinning.

But like I said, there are dozens of passages pointing to God's grace and love, even if we do continually sin. Take a moment to read the parables in the first few books of the New Testament. Jesus uses these parables to explain God's love for us even when we stray and want to return. For example, the one about the son, who left his father's home to participate in heavy drinking and sexual sin with prostitutes. Once the son hit rock bottom and realized he was wrong, he returned home and found his father waiting with open arms for him. His father even threw a feast because he returned home.

I think that we as believers can agree it is never too late to turn your life around. It is never too late to accept Christ into your life or get back into fellowship with him. A perfect example is the story of one of the criminals, who was crucified next to Jesus. While one criminal mocked Jesus on the cross, the other believed in Christ right before he died, so Jesus accepted him. "But the other criminal protested. 'Don't you fear God even when you have been sentenced to die? We deserve to die for our crimes, but this man hasn't done anything wrong.' Then he said, 'Jesus, remember me when you come into your kingdom.' And Jesus replied, 'I assure you; Today, you will be with me in paradise'" (Luke 23:40-43). It is so awesome that the Lord's mercy and grace stems right up to the very last minute of our lives.

In the end, eternity is a long time. I love Jesus with all my heart. I believe I wasn't put on Earth to make it to Heaven—I am here to give glory to God and preach the good news about Jesus Christ. I do these things both with my words and more importantly, in the way I live. Making it to Heaven is a result and reward for doing God's will, and it is nothing I gloat about. I just thank God for the calling He's given me life and the patience He has for me, while I do his will. I pray that everyone will understand his or her purpose in life. I know my purpose doesn't include being tied down by lust or shackled by porn and masturbation. I love the Heavenly Father, Jesus Christ, and the Holy Spirit and am tired of displeasing God. The false high I felt when watching porn and masturbating, isn't even worth the thought of tampering with my salvation.

I feel the need to inform you…

We must constantly feed our spirits or our flesh will take over. We must constantly be in a state of seeking Christ. Yesterday's prayer isn't enough for today. Yesterday's praise and worship isn't going to cut it for today. Yesterday's time in the Word has no impact on today's battles. Our time with the Lord is like eating. We must eat to not be hungry. We must eat to satisfy our bodies. Yesterday's dinner is not going to satisfy your belly today. As believers, we must feed on God every single day. The great thing about spending daily time with the Lord, shifts from what can feel like a Christian duty to a burning desire to be in his presence.

Chapter 8: Fighting the Worldly Current

Being a believer and follower of Christ is not easy. It takes sacrificing yourself, giving up everything in the world. Jesus talks about this in the book of Luke: "If you want to be my disciple, you must, by comparison, hate everyone else—your father and mother, wife and children, brothers and sisters—yes, even your own life. Otherwise, you cannot be my disciple. And if you do not carry your own cross and follow me, you cannot be my disciple" (Luke 14:26-27). Then the very first sentence of verse 28 says, "But don't begin until you count the cost."

There are a lot of people who say they believe in Christ, but they have no interest or desire to live the righteous way Jesus did. Why? Because it is much easier to follow the way of the world. This world is drowning in sin. Our flesh is going to die because of sin. Just like how one plus one equals two, a sinful world plus a sinful flesh equals death for both. It is always going to equal death. Because of this, sinning is like riding a wave. For most of us, there is no resistance when we ride the wave. But following Christ is like turning around and fighting the wave's movement and the current that is flowing towards death and destruction.

That is how I felt when it came to porn; I was fighting against the current. Heavy waves were ramming into me, trying to get my head below water. I was fighting weekly, daily, hourly. Somedays, I would entertain the thought of not fighting. Battered with metaphorical bumps and bruises, those days were difficult. It seemed easier to just turn around and ride the current with the rest of the world. Other days, it seemed even easier to grab a surfboard and really ride the waves. But what we don't realize as we're being hit with the wave is that the wave eventually ends.

That current runs out and eventually leads to an abyss of total darkness. It eventually leads to death and destruction.

Yes, in my past, I have grabbed my surfboard and enjoyed the waves. Not because that is truly what I wanted to do or because it was fun, even though it was. I did it because it was easier to give into my flesh and this world than keep my eyes on God. I have accepted defeat before. In periods of my addiction, I have allowed Satan to convince me that porn and lustfulness was just the way of life. But in those moments that I had given up, God pulled on me although I pushed way His Word. My heart would get heavy, but the Holy Spirit strengthens me, so on days that I remembered to fight, I would tell myself that this is not what God had planned for me. I am not defeated; I am more than a conqueror. I have to fight.

So, I put on my metaphorical swimming goggles, strapped on my flippers, and swam. I do this each time I feel temptation from Satan. I have to swim up to those few people who are also fighting the current. I have to team up with them, so we can push and motivate each other because we know that eventually we will reach land...a true paradise. We will be greeted by the King of Kings and Lord of Lords. We will shed those wet clothes that were weighing us down and be given new clothes; clothes that won't tear, rip, stain, or shrink. God will show us this through His love, forgiveness, mercy, and grace. I need that. I need those new clothes. That is why I have to keep swimming.

At the end of the day, the root of all addictions is a spiritual issue. All strongholds on a person are the enemy trying to keep us from having victory in our lives. In some cases, it is the enemy tricking us into thinking that the addiction is victory. For addictions such as alcoholism, the world has consequences set in place. There are laws to discipline and help deter people from serving them. There are classes and research done to educate people on the consequences of alcohol addiction. The physical and mental effects are also well documented. There are treatment facilities and recovery centers stationed all throughout the country, to help alcoholics fight their addiction. Someone struggling with alcoholism, definitely has numerous resources to turn to.

But what help is there for porn addiction? Can I check myself in at the local hospital and say, "I need help. I've been addicted to porn for 15 years, and it is tearing my soul apart. I have consumed porn four times today, and if I don't get treatment, I will consume more and more." The nurse would look at me like I'm crazy. She might even call security to have me escorted out. Why? Because porn is accepted, or at least tolerated, in our society. It is part of life. For many people, this is what they do when they are bored, sad, feeling lonely, or when their spouse won't have sex with them. Some people do it to start their day and it becomes part of their daily routine. I know because I was one of them. I used to think there was no better way to start the day than to watch some porn and masturbate because there really wasn't anything to help me beat my addiction.

When you want to be healed, you recognize that porn addiction has nothing to do with the visual images you see. It has nothing to do with the feeling of masturbating. That is what initially traps you. But it has everything to do with your fleshly desire to sin. It has everything to do with Satan using that addiction against you. Finding God and receiving the Holy Spirit made me see that I wasn't alone. With God's help, I could break the stronghold of porn.

All those years ago, I wish I had never disobeyed my
parents and snuck downstairs to watch TV. I wish that I
didn't lie and tell my mom I was sick, so I could stay home
and play video games in seventh grade. That terrible day is
what really started the yearning for porn. That day is what
made the demon come alive in me. That day is when sin
against my body took hold of me. That day in seventh
grade, is when I walked out of fellowship with God.

These last few years have been hell. And the decade before
that was hell, too—I just didn't know it at the time. I feel
like I have been suffering for so long. Lord, when are you
going to take these shackles of porn off me? When are you
going to release me from the bondage of lust? I don't want
it anymore. It is eating me up inside. The weight of it is
crushing me. I have been defeated by this more times than I
can count. Why, Father God, must I continue to suffer with
this? Why must my day be interrupted with the thought of
pornography? Why must I go to church to only come home
and sin? Why must my dreams be littered with filth? I don't
want it anymore. I hate it! Porn has made me miserable.
There is nothing rewarding about this. Nothing feels good
anymore. Lord Jesus, please take this sickness from me. It
is not just an addiction. It is a repulsive sickness. I am ill
and I just need an ounce of your healing.

I feel like the woman in the book of Luke, who suffered
twelve years of constant bleeding. She knew if she could
touch Jesus's robe, she would be healed—and she was. I
just need to touch your robe, Jesus. Even if my pinky finger
grazes the smallest piece of your robe, I know I will be
healed. Like the blind man who knew Jesus was passing by,
and he needed healing. I am that blind man: "Jesus, Son of
David, have mercy on me!" (Luke 18:38) I don't care what
the world thinks. I don't care what the world says. I'll shout
louder. "Jesus, Son of David, have mercy on me!" (Luke

18:38) I know you are there. I can feel your presence. You've come to my dreams and told me not to worry. You have blessed me with the gift of the Holy Spirit. Now I need the gift of victory. I need it now. Right now! Tomorrow is too late. I need it now!

I feel the need to confess that....

I would hate to get to heaven and see one of my friends and have one of these encounters:

> Me: Hey man, it's good to see you.
>
> Friend: Hey Ryan! It's good to see you too. I'm glad you made it.
>
> Friend: Where are you staying?
>
> Me: Uhhh over there on "Just Made It Way" in those apartments.
>
> Me: Apartment 3C actually.
>
> Friend: Oh ok
>
> Me: Beau- beautiful apartments.
>
> Friend: Hey it's heaven so I'm sure it is. I'm sure it is.
>
> Friend: Well if you're free later, there's a big banquet being held at my place. I stay over at the Righteous Living Estates.
>
> Me: Oh. Ok

Chapter 9: Victory

I have a friend who dealt with porn for some time. Like me, he has some stories of how bad it was for him. He told me how God set him free. He told me that one day, he told God that he will never watch porn again if the desire of it would go away. Next thing you know, he was healed. The fleshly desire to watch porn and masturbate was gone, and I believe him. I've known this man for almost half my life, and I have never seen him fall under the trap of porn. He told me this story a few times because I could confide in him. His story is a great testimony of God's wonderful works, but although, I was happy for him, I couldn't understand why God couldn't heal me, too. I have put in what I thought was a lot of time trying to be healed and was still in a daily heavyweight fight, exchanging blow for blow with my flesh. However, victory didn't come for me until I submitted myself completely to God. I felt it took longer than it needed for me to get healed because I was trying to do things Ryan's way. I wanted to have God help and bless me the way I wanted to be helped and blessed. I couldn't get out of my own way even for the Lord.

I feel the need to add that...

I believe that much of our problem as Christians is that we spend our entire lives trying to do our own will. We try to achieve our own goals and we want God to bless us, while we do what we want to do. Never mind what he wants us to do. Even though one of the main reasons we are put on this earth is to do the Lord's will. This is why I believe a lot of our blessings are delayed or when we do get blessed, we end up settling for less because if we did it God's way, He would have so much more in store for us. God's blessing is not always about money. Unless we are sick and need healing, the only thing we usually want is our finances taken care of and God is so much bigger than just money. But that is a topic for another day.

My healing began when I stepped aside and let God truly control my life. I wanted to take the shortcut to my healing and victory over porn. I wanted to just pray, read the Word a little, and maybe do a short fast, so I could call myself healed. But that isn't how God operates. He is not a God of shortcuts. God is thorough. God is detailed. God is patient. Now, I'm not saying God was making me sin to prove a point because that is certainly not the God I serve. But he had a bigger purpose for me than simply being healed. The calling He has on my life required me to give myself completely over to Him, so He could heal and build me up in a way that would make me ready for what happens after the healing. Being healed and delivered from porn wasn't the end of this journey; it was the beginning.

So what does giving the keys over to God look like? Well, the first thing I had to do was simply get out of the way. For me, this meant fasting. Fasting is something I struggle with because I love to eat. Food tastes so good. I'm a meat eater and could eat a juicy steak or slow-roasted chicken wings every day. Unfortunately, feeding my flesh gave it strength to want to do evil, which meant I had to weaken my flesh. Although I was strengthening my spirit throughout the whole process of being healed, my flesh was constantly getting fed. Literally. I noticed that every time I had food in me, my flesh was pushing me to watch porn. It became really hard to defeat. But when I was hungry and weak, my fleshly urge to sexually sin was minimal and sometimes nonexistent. That is what fasting is: weakening the flesh so we can better seek God's wisdom and turning our focus from our body to the Lord.

When Jesus went into the wilderness to be tempted by Satan, what was the very first thing Satan tempted him with? It was food! "For forty days and forty nights, he fasted and became very hungry. During that time, the Devil came and said to him, "If you are the Son of God, tell these stones to become loaves of bread" (Matthew 4:2-3). Why did Satan tempt him with food first? Because Satan knew if he could strengthen Jesus's flesh, it would make it more difficult for Jesus to resist future temptations. Jesus would be fighting both his flesh and Satan. Obviously, Satan failed with this tactic, but if he used this strategy against Jesus, he surely would try it on us.

Let me explain from another angle. Suppose you are weak from lack of food, and your greatest enemy approaches you. This enemy has every intention to harm you. The last thing this enemy is trying to do is feed you, which would give you physical strength. In the natural world, we can make sense of this, food equals strength for our flesh. But Satan doesn't operate in the natural world. He operates in the supernatural world. Satan was not trying to feed Jesus, so He could have the strength to survive. Satan was trying to feed Jesus, so he could interrupt his spiritual connection with God. We fast for many reasons but the major reason we fast is to weaken our flesh, so we can hear God better. We starve our flesh, so it will submit to our spirit. And we replace our mealtime with time in the Lord's presence. This is exactly what Jesus was doing and what Satan was trying to stop from happening. As the Bible says, "For we are not fighting against flesh and blood enemies but against evil rulers and authorities of the unseen world: against mighty powers in this dark world and against evil spirits in the heavenly places" (Ephesians 6:12).

One night, I was just ending a three-day water fast. I needed to get closer to God. I needed to hear His voice. I

60

needed to separate myself from my flesh and all the sin that comes with it. I was lying in bed, having just eaten my first meal, since ending my fast and it didn't take long until the thoughts of porn started. I was so mad and couldn't ignore them because if I did, one of three things would happen: (1) I would have a long night wrestling with these sinful thoughts: (2) my dreams that night would be a lust fest: (3) the following night, those thoughts would come back twice as strong. I've been there dozens of times. Eventually, I was going to give in. If it wasn't the second or third night, it would be the fourth or fifth night. So, on this particular night, I did something different. I got down on my hands and knees, but I didn't ask God to get these thoughts out of my head. I told him instead. I said, "God, you see me struggling. You see what's in my mind. I need you to remove it NOW!" I called upon Jesus in the same prayer. I said, "Jesus, you see what's in my mind. You see the thoughts. I need them gone NOW! Amen." I got up off my knees, and before I could lay in my bed, the thoughts were gone. What a great God we serve!

I felt I was no longer chained to porn after my church's 21-day fast. Every year, my church does the "Daniel fast," which is basically just eating fruits, vegetables, whole grains, and drinking water. I tried this fast the year before and had fallen short, lasting maybe five days. When the next year rolled around, I was committed to completing the fast.

Fasting does nothing for God. When we fast, it doesn't make God greater; He is already infinitely great. Fasting does everything for us. When it comes to fasting, the Bible uses the word "when" not "if," which means it's not if you fast, it's when you fast. Jesus says, "And when you fast, don't make it obvious, as the hypocrites do, for they try to look miserable and disheveled so people will admire them

61

for their fasting" (Matthew 6:16). Some demons, strongholds, or issues in life can only be cured with prayer and fasting. Let me say that again. Some sins can only be cured with prayer and fasting.

When Jesus sent his disciples to heal the sick and cast out demons, they came across a demon-possessed boy. The evil spirit often harmed the boy by throwing him into water and fire. The boy would fall on the ground, foam at the mouth, and grind his teeth. This demon really had a hold on this boy's life and was trying to kill this child. Jesus's disciples tried to cast out the demon but failed to do so. This caused a scene, and a large crowd grew around them. Jesus eventually showed up and removed the evil spirit from the boy. The Bible says that, "Afterward, when Jesus was alone in the house with his disciples, they asked, 'Why couldn't we cast out that evil spirit?' Jesus replied, 'This kind can be cast out only by prayer and fasting'" (Mark 9:28-29). Porn was my demon. I'm not afraid to admit it. I had a demon attached to me. I would wrestle that demon all day and night, and eventually, he would always conquer me. I've said dozens of prayers over the years. I've said, "In Jesus name" more than I can count. I've watched sermons and have gotten down on my knees to plead with the Lord. But this demon was one that could only be conquered with prayer and fasting.

The sad part is I knew that. I just wasn't willing to put the work in. I was in denial. I thought there was another way to get this wickedness off of me. I really wanted God to do everything. God wouldn't do His part until I did mine. I had to take up my cross and follow Jesus to Calvary, for the Bible says, "Then Jesus said to his disciples, 'If any of you wants to be my follower, you must give up your own way, take up your cross, and follow me'" (Matthew 16:24).

I'm not going to lie to you…fasting for 21 days is not easy. It takes a desire to want to be closer to God and hear His voice. It takes a strong desire to be healed. Fasting takes a lot out of your flesh. But that's good! I knew I wanted and needed to be healed. I knew each time I submitted to porn, I was delaying God's plan for me. So, it began. The first two or three days are always the toughest. I kept telling my flesh to shut up. I set aside at least an hour to spend time in prayer each day after work. I woke up at least 30 minutes early to read his Word. Additionally, I turned my morning prayer from a 30-second rehearsed monologue to a 10-minute call to God. I decided I wasn't going to eat until after six each evening. So, during lunch at work, instead of eating, I used that time for fellowship with Him. On the weekends, I spent even more time in prayer and worship. I had to do some extreme altering to my life because I needed extreme results. I needed a miracle!

Before I continue, I want to say there are certain things that are between God and his children. He reveals certain things to some and not others. This is intentional. Jesus says, "But when you pray, go away by yourself, shut the door behind you, and pray to your Father in private. Then your Father, who sees everything, will reward you" (Matthew 6:6). What Christ is saying is go one on one with God. When you are one on one with Him, He will reward you and the reward is not some material thing. The reward is more of him. That's why Jesus said go in private, so nobody else sees what He is about to do in your life. Jesus says shut the door behind you because what He is about to do is only meant for you.

Everything God does is not meant for everyone to see. In Exodus 19:20 God says, "The Lord came down on top of Mount Sinai and called Moses to the top of the mountain. So Moses climbed the mountain." God didn't call his cousin, Aaron who was the spokesman for Moses to join along. He didn't call Moses's wife or children or any of the priests. God called just him. It was a private meeting for only Moses to witness. So forgive me if I don't go in great detail of everything I'm about to mention. I pray this encourages you to seek after the Lord more, so you can also have these breathtaking experiences.

Day four was the first time I felt like I was defeating porn for good this time. I was watching a little TV before bed, and while I was sitting there, a bombardment of porn images suddenly pounded my mind. They just came in boat loads, one after another, and it happened so fast that I didn't have time to rebuke, or dismiss, them. I didn't have time to do anything! I haven't had a temptation like that before. It felt like I was a boxer in the ring - me and the enemy. I felt like I was starting to get the enemy on the ropes but then he gave me a 20-punch combination, all with the strength Mike Tyson shows in the ring. If this had happened before the fast, I would have thrown in the towel and said, "It's a wrap. Sorry, Lord. Forgive me. I'll do better next time." But I gritted my teeth and absorbed all those blows, smiling because I wasn't fazed by it. Satan knew his defeat was drawing near and threw everything he had at me. I was still looking at the TV, but in my mind, I was thanking the Lord for helping me get through that.

Having previously fallen short of completing the 21 day "Daniel fast," I noticed this time felt different. Day six was the day I felt the presence of the Lord. I felt a shift in the atmosphere, like the Lord was in the room. It reminded me of the day I received the Holy Spirit and it was a glorious moment. I wouldn't be giving God any justice if I tried to explain the beauty of it. But I will say this… Never mind, I can't put it into words. It was awesome!

Some people like to spend their time in prayer and worship in complete silence. I do that too. Like every morning I pray in silence. I pray throughout my day in silence but when the workday is done, and I have no obligations, I have a concert-like setting in my home. I call it prayer and worship time. I have worship music blasting either in my headphones or through the TV and sound bar. It helps me to block out the noise and really get dialed in with the Lord. I highly recommend this to everyone. Even if you live at home with your parents, have a house full of kids, or have roommates, don't let that stop you from worshiping the Lord. It's an excuse. Go into your closet if you must. Close the door, and worship the Lord, for the Bible says, "But when you pray, go away by yourself, shut the door behind you, and pray to your Father in private. Then your Father, who sees everything, will reward you" (Matthew 6:6). The true reward is being in the presence of the Lord. He will break you down and build you up the right way.

While I was fasting, I kept hearing friends and family talk about how they wanted the fast to be over. How they were craving food. Even people who weren't fasting would talk about how they couldn't give up this food or that meal. I'm not knocking them for it because in the past, I was one of them. But prayer and fasting are bigger than just a hungry stomach. People just zoom in on the fasting and they are not fully understanding. They fail to realize that fasting without prayer is nothing but a diet and a waste of time when it comes to our spiritual being. Fasting will weaken the flesh but it's the prayer that shifts the spiritual battle in our favor. Prayer positions us to hear the Lord. Prayer changes our mindset. Prayer is powerful. Prayer is a weapon against the enemy.

If day six of the fast was the start of the awesomeness, day nine had to be even more awesome. My evening prayer and worship time became complete surrender to the Lord. I'm talking my spirit took over within 10 minutes of me praying. I pray all believers in Christ get to experience the things the Lord has done in my life.

Prayer is not a one-way street. Prayer is not us just telling God our problems and how we need this in our lives or we need things to go away. Prayer is not even all about giving God the glory. While He deserves all the glory and praise, prayer is communication with the Lord. Prayer is connecting to the spiritual world to get results on Earth. Also, when we pray, our prayers need to be in line with what God's Word says, which is stated in James 4:2-3 "… Yet you don't have what you want because you don't ask God for it. And even when you ask, you don't get it because your motives are all wrong—you want only what will give you pleasure."

When I read the Bible, especially the old testament, it seems like God was talking daily to people. Moses, Abraham, Joshua, David, Jeremiah… The list goes on and on. I kept wondering why I wasn't getting to have conversations with God. I have learned two things though: God Is talking to us through his Word and that God does speak. God is talking all the time. But we have to position ourselves to hear His voice. This was confirmed on day 12 of my fast. I will spare you the details but it was epic.

During each day of fasting and prayer, I grew more spiritual. I felt I was being made new in His presence. The main reason I did this fast was to break completely from porn. I had a few other desires I wanted, but my main focus was deliverance from porn. By day 15, I forgot that I was doing the fast because of my porn addiction. When I was in prayer, I would forget to pray about it. I forgot because it was no longer an issue for me. It was no longer hovering over me like a dark cloud; it was just gone. The burden had been lifted.

Let me put it this way. If someone has perfect 20/20 vision, if he's never needed glasses, never struggled to see and never had any problems with his eyes, why would he spend his prayer time praying about having healthy eyes? He already has them, so why pray about it? In summary, I forgot to pray about porn because there was nothing to pray about. I had been delivered.

Day 20. The near end of this monumental experience. I always like to say God doesn't just show up; He shows out. When God is near us, the outcome is greater than what any human could think of. During my fasting and praying, I told the Lord that I knew He was going to do something awesome before it was over. Sure enough, on day 20, He did. I beg of you, though, please take the time to be alone with the Lord and watch what He will do. When I say that, I'm not talking about what He will do in terms of blessing you with things. I'm talking about what He will do at that very moment. He will reveal things to you that would make some believers doubt. God is an awesome God!

.

Day 21. The Holy Spirit is real my friends. Just as the Word of God says, the Holy Spirit is indeed a comforter, an advocate, a counselor and an encourager. "And the Holy Spirit helps us in our weakness. For example, we don't know what God wants us to pray for. But the Holy Spirit prays for us with groaning that cannot be expressed in words" (Romans 8:26). On that day, I experienced the fullness of the Holy Spirit. It was a life changing phenomenon. I hope all my brothers and sisters in Christ gain the fullness of the Holy Spirit. It is darn near impossible to operate without Him.

I don't have the perfect solution to fix a porn addiction. I don't have a 12-step program people should follow to beat the bondage of sexual sin. I don't have the key to success. But I do know who does. I do know who conquers all things. I do know whose name is above every name and would be glad to point you in His direction. I would be glad to take my cross up with you, as we follow Him together to the place many thought was defeat, even though it is truly victory.

Temptation will always be there. The enemy is always going to try and tempt us. The fasting and praying I did never stopped the temptations of porn. I was just so in line with God that they had no effect on me. Graphic images still came but walking with the Lord dissolved those images. The apostle Paul says, "If we live in the Spirit, let us also walk in the Spirit" (*King James Version,* Galatians 5:25). It's interesting that he uses the word "walk." That means constant movement...that we should never stop being in the presence of the Lord. We all have to continue to pray and seek Christ, while reading his Word. We have to walk with Him because the moment we stop, we distance ourselves from God and in that moment, temptation will defeat us.

I feel the need to admit…

I give myself no credit for any good I have done in my life. All glory goes to God. I've come to the conclusion that all I do is get in the way of what the Lord is trying to do in my life. You know when the apostle Paul says think thoughts that come from the spirit. Well, I love thinking spirit filled thoughts and I give myself no credit for that. My friend and I were talking about something going on in pop culture and he asked me how I felt about it. I answered with the straightest and most sincere face and I told him "all I'm focused on is serving the Lord." And I meant it. I wasn't saying it like it was a cliche. I really meant it and I felt good to say something about the Lord that had nothing but truth behind it. And once again, I give myself zero credit for it. God's patience, his mercy and grace are the only reason I'm breathing today. God is really showing me my purpose in life and it feels good to have a God filled purpose. God is using me! Who am I to be used? I am nothing but a sinner saved by grace.

Chapter 10: Keep Pressing Forward

While you are overcoming porn, you might fall. Honestly, you probably will fall a few times. If you have been buried in it for years like me, you have a lot of digging to do. The road to cleansing and healing is not easy, but the reward is better than anything you will ever get. The worst thing I, or any of us, could do is give up. That is exactly what the enemy wants us to do. He wants you to throw in the towel and accept defeat. He wants you to accept the false notion that you can't overcome porn. Don't listen to him! Giving up is worse than sinning with porn. Giving up means you have turned your back on God. It means you have given up on God. It means you don't believe Christ has set you free from the power of sin, which means everything you have read in the Bible is false. That is absolutely not the case, though!

Also, do not fall victim to trying to manage your porn. It is another way of accepting defeat. First off, if you think managing how much porn or sin you commit in a given time is better than just sinning whenever you feel like it, you are sadly mistaken. Sin is sin. Having a schedule or cap on how much porn you watch per week is still sin. It is still wicked and wrong. Also, I challenge anyone, who is struggling with a porn addiction to successfully try and manage his or her sin alone. It is impossible to think you are going to tell your flesh when and how much sin to commit. I promise that you won't last a week. If you give the Devil an inch, he will take a mile every time.

If you say, "I'm only going to watch porn once a day, that's it." I guarantee by day three you will be watching porn more than once a day. Porn management is not a step in the right direction. It is a waste of time. It is delaying the inevitable of you watching porn multiple times a day. Porn management is a fluffy way of accepting defeat. You are telling yourself and God that you submit to porn but only for a limited time every day. That is comical to think that way. Please show me in Scripture where someone managed his sin. Show me where Jesus said it is okay to manage sin. Please do not try to manage porn. It is an impossible feat.

The truth is that the harder sin is to overcome means the bigger the breakthrough is going to be. Your struggle will help someone else not struggle. Your victory will bring victory to others. God has put a calling on your life, and as a living witness, I am here to tell you it's not to be consumed by porn. The Bible says, "The Lord isn't really being slow about his promise, as some people think. No, he is being patient for your sake. He does not want anyone to be destroyed but wants everyone to repent" (2 Peter 3:9).

During the Last Supper, Jesus explained what was going to happen to him in the coming hours to all his disciples. Then, Jesus looked at Peter, whose name used to be Simon, and said, "'Simon, Satan has asked to sift each of you like wheat. But I have pleaded in prayer for you, Simon, that your faith should not fail. So, when you have repented and turned to me again, strengthen your brothers'" (Luke 22:31-32). Peter loved Jesus. He believed in him and thought he wasn't going to fold under pressure. Peter replied to Jesus, "'Lord, I am ready to go to prison with you and even to die with you.' But Jesus said, 'Peter, let me tell you something. Before the rooster crows tomorrow morning, you will deny three times that you even know me'" (Luke 22:33-34). Sure enough, Peter did exactly what Jesus said he would do. The Bible says, "At that moment, the Lord turned and looked at Peter. Suddenly, the Lord's words flashed through Peter's mind: 'Before the rooster crows tomorrow morning, you will deny three times that you even know me.' And Peter left the courtyard, weeping bitterly" (Luke 22:61-62).

I feel like this could be Jesus talking to me about my lusting. Let's substitute my name with Peter's and change the topic of "denying Jesus" to "lusting". Jesus would have told me, "Ryan, you will lust three times before you even seek me." I would quickly tell Jesus, "No, I will not lust. Even if I was forced into a sexual environment, I would seek you before I gave into lust. My faith in you, Jesus, is strong. I love you, Jesus. I am not that lust-filled man anymore. Even with my back against the wall, I will not lust." Like Peter in the heat of the night, I would fall short and lust.

The beauty of Jesus is that he forgives. He knows we mean well. He knows our hearts. He knows where we fall short and struggle. That's why Jesus told Peter, "'I have pleaded in prayer for you.'" Jesus pleads for us to the Father daily. The most important thing Jesus said to Peter was to repent and then go lift up his brethren. So, if you fall short, repent and then encourage those around you. We cannot defeat porn alone. We cannot conquer lust by ourselves. We need Jesus. We need Him every step of the way, and if we stumble, that is when we need Him most of all. Jesus knows us inside and out and loves us despite our sin.

Before Paul was the Apostle Paul, he was Saul of Tarsus. The man, who wrote a good chunk of the new testament was hailing Christians in jail at one point. He didn't believe anything about Jesus. One day, on his way to Damascus with intentions of bringing Christians back to Jerusalem in chains, Saul had an encounter with Jesus. To summarize, Jesus shows Saul that He does exist. Jesus blinds Saul for a few days, heals him, and then converts him to Paul. You can find this whole story in Acts:9 Think about this: The

Apostle Paul was once the enemy. He was once against God and a very wicked man. Paul did things in his past that I'm sure could have been easily used as ammunition for Satan. I'm sure there were times Satan tried to remind him of what he used to be. But Jesus saved him. Jesus not only saved him, but he also used him. Jesus not only used him, but he made Paul a staple figure in the living Word of God. That is amazing. After everything Paul had been through, the one thing he mentions that he has grabbed a hold of is forgetting the past, for he says, "No, dear brothers and sisters, I have not achieved it, but I focus on this one thing: forgetting the past and looking forward to what lies ahead" (Philippians 3:13). That's powerful. Take that with you, my brothers and sisters in Christ. The past is the past. Satan is going to try to keep you there. Don't let him. Keep pressing forward.

I have faith that you will beat this addiction. I have faith you will be victorious. Don't give up. Victory is already yours—you just have to take it. Go, claim what God has already promised you, and don't stop fighting until you win. The Bible says, "Take possession of the land, and settle in it because I have given it to you to occupy" (Numbers 33:53). This Scripture stems from when God had already rescued Israel from slavery. God told Moses to tell the people of Israel to drive out all the people in the land of Canaan and claim it for themselves. This scripture says God told Moses the land is theirs, which means victory is already theirs. Even though God gave them victory, they still needed to fight the enemy to claim the victory God had already promised them. It is the same with porn, or any sinful addiction. God has already given you victory over it but you still need to fight to claim that victory. I pray for you daily. Please pray for me as well. I know it's tough sometimes but remember that you are healed. In the name of Jesus, you are healed!

Personal Acknowledgements

I've kept my struggle with porn a secret. Only a few people knew what I was going through. They were my brothers in Christ, Kevin and Demarcus. I want to thank you both for the role you played in my life, while I was dealing with the bondage of porn. Whether it was a simple conversation we had, a prayer we shared, or just leading by example, it made an impact on my life. Thank you for your unwavering friendship!

I would also like to thank Minister Mack for being responsive to the Holy Spirit. For several days, I was asking the Lord what He wanted me to do. I felt like I had a purpose and a mission I was supposed to achieve but didn't know what it was. I remember one Sunday morning, I was sitting in Church, and God told me I was going to write a book. I was like, "Okay, a book? What is this book going to be about?" He told me it was going to be about me overcoming porn. I was so happy God answered my prayers and told me my assignment. Later during that same service, Minister Mack was preaching and confirmed God's plan for me. While preaching, he briefly shifted his topic on "being kingdom minded" to talking about when writing a book, it is best to start with an outline. I remember Minister Mack said, "That's for somebody." Well, that somebody was me.

To Royce Dickson, my big brother. Growing up, I always wanted to follow in his footsteps and I found myself having an interest in everything he did. I always admired his massive shoe inventory, collection of cool cars and occasionally would sneak in his room to borrow an outfit or two. He was the best player on our high school football team and I would take pride in knowing that it was my brother, who was undoubtedly the most popular kid in school. Royce is and has always been a go-getter and when he is determined to have something, it will inevitably be his. Royce, I've watched you overcome some of the worst of situations life can throw at you, which has taught me to always keep my head held high and never let anyone or anything stand in my way. Thank you for being a role model, and the true definition of "my brother's keeper". Although I don't verbalize it, you know I've always been your biggest fan and I know that God will bless you with all the desires of your heart. Continue to seek the Lord, keep him first and remember God is in the midst of it! I Love you suck butt

To Taylar Dickson, or as I like to call her "Dr. Tay Tay," the oldest of my baby sisters. I have distinct memories of her in high school and the countless hours she spent studying, long into the midnight hours. From a young age, I knew she'd be exceptional in whatever she put her hands to and I was excited to watch where her God-given focus would lead her. I'm extremely proud to say that today, she is a medical student in pursuit of a career that would meet people at their worst, and through God's immense powers, offer physical and emotional healing. As my sister, I want to thank her for her years of fun, football, and our fair share of fights. But even more, I want to thank her for her studious and driven spirit. She is a beautiful young woman of God, who showed me the importance of pursuing my goals no matter how difficult or far off they seemed. I thank her for being an example of God's Love, and the zealous determination He imparts in us all, to advance His Kingdom through our divine purpose. I love you!

To Tylar Dickson, my other little sister. I sure can't acknowledge "Dr. Tay Tay" if I didn't acknowledge "Mrs. Ty". Ty has always been my free-spirited sister. She works hard but doesn't ignore her social-butterfly duties. Her playful and humorous spirit always makes me laugh and I admire her courage for always delving into new adventures. She is full of ambition and although sometimes too self-critical, she never forgets how she looks through the eyes of the Lord. I respect how she takes life one day at a time and pushes her God given purpose. She stays strong in faith and patiently waits for God to reveal his plans for her. Thank you for showing me that life doesn't have to be rushed and that we all need a break from its stresses sometimes. Thank you for carving out time in your busy schedule, for our nights on call or duty or Sunday afternoons watching the Lions. Thank you for exemplifying what it means to wait in faith and for never being discouraged from going after what God has for you. Lastly, thank you for being the other half of our "younger siblings rule" group. I love you!

To my father, Barry Dickson. From all of the memories of my dad, the one that sticks out to me most is his undesirable love for football. He was my reason for playing little league and in high school. He instilled in me my unwavering love for the Detroit Lions and I cherished the time we got to watch games together. I always looked forward to our annual draft parties at his house and the opportunity to just sit and discuss with him the intricateness of the sport. The bond we shared over football is unmatched. Like any football team, my dad has faced many ups and downs but he's always refused to stay down. I admired his hard-working and never quit attitude. Thank you for always pushing forward through all of your hardship and showing me what it looks like to strive for the Lord, throughout a time of struggle. I love you!

To my dear mother, Shawn Dickson. I would be remiss to not spend a considerable amount of time thanking the most influential woman I've encountered in my life. From the very start, my mother has shown unwavering courage and strength. I've watched her overcome almost unworldly struggles, all for the sake of her children, whom she would move mountains and give her last for. My mother is an earthly example of God's incomprehensible love and will to sacrifice for others. She would always tell us that helping others won't always be at our convenience and that we must be willing to do whatever we can, whenever we have the opportunity to share God's Love. This lesson followed me well into my adulthood and I found joy in blessing others for the sake of the Kingdom. I want to thank her for unconditional love, prayers, and support throughout my life and during the process of developing this book. I want to thank her for instilling in me a love for people and the importance of truly loving my neighbor. My mother and I share a unique, unbreakable bond. I take pride in being her "baby boy" and revel in being referred to as a "momma's boy." She had a habit of peaking over my shoulder, as I typed away at this book and inquired often about the

content. I answered all of her curious questions with, "You'll see when it's published, Momma!" So Momma, this is for you.
Love forever, your little Ry Ry

To my editor, Patricia Barthwell, aka, "Auntie Trish," for her due diligence and commitment to making sure I produced a final product that showed my truth and my authentic self. When I contacted her for this project, she did not hesitate to commit, nor did she ever place any judgement on my subject matter. Thank you for your encouragement and for believing in me!

****

Last, but not least, I give all praise, glory, and honor to my Heavenly Father God, Jesus Christ, and the Holy Spirit. The love you have for me is matched by no man. The mercy and grace you show me daily cannot be comprehended in the human mind.

To all the readers:

I hope my story helps you on your journey with Christ as well. May the Lord be with you now and always.

I love you all.

Thank you.

On June 6, 2020, Ryan Donovan Dickson fulfilled his earthly purpose and departed this life. His 27 years were spent seeking the Lord and growing deeper in his faith. During his lifetime, Ryan truly enriched his biblical knowledge and his intimate relationship with the Lord. He is now happily resting in God's glory!
His memory and legacy will live on through his family and loved ones.

www.ingramcontent.com/pod-product-compliance
Lightning Source LLC
Chambersburg PA
CBHW032027040426
42448CB00006B/747